THE

FIVE GREAT MYSTERIES

IN THE BIBLE

WITNESS LEE

Living Stream Ministry
Anaheim, CA

First Edition, September 1999.

ISBN 0-7363-0711-7

Published by

Living Stream Ministry
2431 W. La Palma Ave., Anaheim, CA 92801 U.S.A.
P. O. Box 2121, Anaheim, CA 92814 U.S.A.

Printed in the United States of America

99   00   01   02   03   04   /   9   8   7   6   5   4   3   2   1

CONTENTS

PREFACE

This book is a translation of messages given in Chinese by Brother Witness Lee in Anaheim, California on February 11-13, 1983.

CHAPTER ONE

THE MYSTERY OF THE UNIVERSE

Scripture Reading: Gen. 1:1; Rom. 1:20; Psa. 19:1-3; 8:1-4; Heb. 1:3; Isa. 40:22; Job 26:7

Praise the Lord that we brothers and sisters who are scattered in the United States and Canada can have a happy reunion here today. We are truly joyful to see the faces of so many dear ones. However, the Lord has given me a heavy burden, and I have been considering what to speak.

THE MYSTERIES BEING MANY

One day a few months ago, I had the inner sense that the universe is a story of mysteries, and the Bible is also a record of mysteries. Then I considered: According to my general knowledge and the knowledge which I have obtained from reading the Bible, how many mysteries are there in the universe? Moreover, how many mysteries are there in the Bible? It is strange that the word *mystery* is not found in the Old Testament; however, it is used again and again in the New Testament. We can probably find ten to twenty different mysteries in the New Testament. For example, Matthew 13 speaks about the mysteries of the kingdom of the heavens.

In the universe, even a mosquito or a bee is a mystery. Not only the animals are mysteries, but the plants also are mysteries. Consider this: Two seeds may look exactly the same, yet after they are sown, one bears white flowers and the other bears yellow flowers. What a mystery! I planted a number of "bird of paradise" plants in my yard. When one day they bloomed, I was shocked. I have been observing the "bird of paradise" flowers for many years. The blooms are golden yellow and blue, with a little white, and the leaves are green.

If we asked even the best Chinese artist to paint with the best colors, he still could not paint something so beautiful. No biologist can tell us why the "bird of paradise" flowers are golden yellow and blue.

Our elderly Brother Weigh, who graduated with a biology major from the Chin-ning University in Nanching, was an expert in raising bees. When I met him for the first time, we spoke about bees. He said, "Brother Lee, bees are very mysterious. Some of them are leaders, some are queens, some are in groups, some are guards, and some are night-watchers. It is really marvelous! They are more submissive than the Chinese wives; some know how to exercise their headship in a way that is superior even to the way we Christians exercise our headship." I was very glad to learn that even the little bee is a mystery.

THE FIVE GREAT MYSTERIES IN THE BIBLE

I have no intention to speak about the mystery of plants or animals; my intention is to speak about the five great mysteries. Bees are a mystery, but they are a small mystery, not a great mystery. Then what are the great mysteries? Of course, the heavens and the earth are the first great mystery, which is also according to the sequence of the Bible. The first two items listed in the record of God's creation are first the heavens and second the earth. How mysterious are the heavens and the earth!

Do you know how big heaven is? More than twenty years ago when I first came to the United States to work for the Lord, I lived in Los Angeles. An observatory there published a report, saying that the sun we see and the nine great planets form one solar system; two hundred forty million solar systems constitute one galaxy; and forty billion galaxies constitute the entire system of the universe. Try to calculate this! Then in 1975 there was a report of a new discovery, saying that one hundred billion galaxies constitute the entire system of the universe. How many can you count? The astronomers claim that their study was very thorough, but I do not believe so. Twenty years ago they said forty billion galaxies form the universe, then after twenty years the number was increased from forty billion to one hundred billion. I am afraid that after another twenty years the number will go up to two hundred billion. The universe is too mysterious; its vastness is a mystery.

There are mainly five great mysteries in the Bible. The first great mystery is the universe, and the second is man. Zechariah 12:1 says, "Jehovah, who stretches forth the heavens and lays the foundations of the earth and forms the spirit of man within him." You should not consider man to be so small. Man is as great as the heavens and the earth, because this verse, after referring to the heavens and the earth, immediately mentions man. Even the Chinese sages considered heaven, earth, and man as three powers. Every one of us is important; we are all very great persons.

Man's greatness is not like the greatness of the universe that lies in its vastness. Man is great in that there is a mystery in him, a mystery which is of three layers. The first layer is the mystery of the body, man's outward part; the second layer is the mystery of the human soul, man's inward part; and the third layer is the mystery of the spirit, man's innermost part.

The third great mystery in the Bible is God. God is too mysterious! The fourth great mystery is Christ, and the fifth is the church. The universe, man, God, Christ, and the church are the five great mysteries shown to us in the Bible. We are humans standing on the earth with the heaven above us; we have God; we are Christians, and we are in the church. We have a share in heaven and earth, in humanity, in God, in Christ, and in the church. Hallelujah, we have a share in each of the five great mysteries!

The Bible is a written explanation of these five great mysteries. We should never think that we are already clear about all these things because we have been Christians for a long time. I have been a Christian for more than half a century and have also read and worn out several Bibles. I feel, however, that I still do not know these five great mysteries in an adequate way. The Bible is a book of mysteries that records in particular the Christian mysteries. These five great mysteries, which are universal facts, require a book of explanation.

The universe is a story of mystery, and the Bible is its explanation. Actually, the explanation of this mystery is found also in the universe itself. We have the universe and the Bible. What is the story of heaven and earth? What is the story of man? What is the story of Christ? And what is the story of the church? All these matters are clearly spoken of in the Bible. I have not delved into many books, but the one book I have read the most is the Holy Bible. The Bible is the unique book, the book of books. Blessed are those who diligently study the Bible!

USING THE BIBLE TO PROVE SCIENCE

In these days there is a group of Christians who are scientists and who love to say, "We will use science to prove the Bible." I do not agree with this kind of saying. Rather, we are in favor of using the Bible to prove science. Any science that does not correspond with the Bible is untenable.

You probably know that many theories are changed after a few years. Science today is different from science fifty years ago; forgive me for saying this. This does not mean that I despise education; rather, I encourage the young people to receive education. However, that is on the human side. God has given us a Bible, which we may now use to measure science.

First, let us consider the origin of the universe. Everyone agrees that this origin is monistic, not pluralistic. Genesis 1:1 says, "In the beginning God created the heavens and the earth." This is monistic; this one beginning is just God Himself. Moreover, the earth created by God is round, not flat or square. There are two portions of the Word to prove this matter.

The Book of Isaiah

Over two thousand seven hundred years ago, near the time of Confucius in China, which was the time of Isaiah in the Old Testament of the Jews, Isaiah said that God sits above the circle of the earth (Isa. 40:22). How interesting it is that Isaiah spoke such a word even near the time of

Confucius! The earth which Isaiah referred to was the earth created by God in the beginning in Genesis 1.

Nearly twenty-seven hundred years after Isaiah, at the time of the translation of the Chinese Bible, because people had the concept of the earth being a globe, the translators rendered this verse as: "It is He who sits upon the circle of the globe." After I read this and did some research on it, I concluded that the word *globe* should not be used. Why? Because at the time of Isaiah, the word *globe* could not be found in any dictionary; only the word *earth* was there. Therefore, I looked into the original language and found that Isaiah 40:22 does not contain the word *globe* but *earth*. If the word *globe* is used, the opposers could say that the Bible is a fabrication. Hence, we dare not use the word *globe*. What Isaiah said was that God is sitting above the circle of the earth.

The Book of Job

Another proof in the Bible can be found in the book of Job. Job lived probably at the time of Abraham, between one and two thousand years earlier than Isaiah. Even at such an ancient time, Job said, "He [God] stretches out the north over the void; / He hangs the earth upon nothing" (Job 26:7). This is really wonderful! Even such an ancient person of about four thousand years ago knew that the earth is hanging upon nothing, which has been confirmed today also by astronomers. Now you can see that it is secure and dependable to use the Bible as a proof of science.

The Book of Genesis

Furthermore, the record in the Bible concerning God's creation occupies only one and a half chapters, Genesis 1 and the first half of Genesis 2. According to the record in Genesis, God first created the lifeless things and then the living things. Among the living things, God first created the life on the lower level, then the life on the middle level, then the life on the higher level, and eventually the life on the highest level. God first created the lifeless things: the earth, the water, the sun, and the air. These four lifeless items are four great necessities of life. Without the earth, water, sunlight, and air, there would be no way for living things to exist.

In your schooling you learned about the expanse surrounding the earth. The Chinese Bible translated the Hebrew word for *expanse* as atmosphere, or air. The atmosphere, the air, surrounding the earth is called the expanse. The word *expanse* means an opening out, a spreading out. If you go to the best English dictionary, it will tell you that this word means to open out, to stretch out, to spread out. I found out that this is also the meaning of the Hebrew word. God said, "Let there be an expanse," and there was an expanse. This expanse separated the waters from the waters. The waters above the expanse were called heaven, and the waters under the expanse were called earth.

Besides the expanse that surrounds the earth, there is no atmosphere or air anywhere else. When humans landed on the moon, they had to bring air with them because there is no expanse around the moon. Now the scientists are still studying whether there is life on Venus. I would say there is also no life on Venus. This is because the living things were created for God's unique purpose, which is to have man as His expression. There are no living things on the moon because neither air nor water can be found there. Therefore, it is very proper to confirm science with the Bible. We do not use science to confirm the Bible; instead, we use the Bible to confirm science.

Let me mention another simple matter. You who are doctors know that the elements of the human body are the same as the elements of dust. Dust contains elements such as copper, iron, sulfur, and phosphorus. Scientific studies confirm that the elements of the human body are simply the elements of dust. However, the Bible already told us long ago that the human body was formed out of dust.

When I was very young, I began to read the Bible. I thought it was something laughable when I read about God's creation of man. I said to myself, "How could it be that God would be like us to use clay to make a little child?" Little did I know that this record is very scientific. There have been many ancient writings, yet not one of them tells us that the human body was made with dust. However, the Bible says, "Jehovah God formed man with the dust of the ground" (Gen. 2:7a). God created man with a mouth and with nostrils. Then He breathed into man's nostrils the breath of life, and man became living and even became a living soul (v. 7b).

Such a record not only corresponds with science, but it also corresponds with Chinese ethics, which does not deal with God but deals with the human soul. God breathed into the nostrils of Adam; then Adam, a man who was made of dust, became a living soul. This living soul is the focus of the study in Chinese ethics. Chinese moralists, from Confucius and Mencius in the ancient time to Wang Yang-ming of the modern age, all studied about the soul. The study of ethics is the study of the human soul. The Chinese moralists found out that there is something in man which they called "bright virtue." The doctrine taught by the Chinese philosophers was the principle of "The Great Learning," which is to develop and enhance the "bright virtue" within man. This corresponds with what the Bible says about the soul. This shows you that the record in the Bible is concise yet profound; it is simple and real yet mysterious. Thus, no one can deny that heaven, earth, and man were created by God. The Bible says so, and science also confirms it.

GOD BEING THE MEANING OF THE UNIVERSE

There must be a meaning to the existence of heaven and earth; all things have a meaning for their existence. What is the meaning of heaven and earth? The meaning of heaven and earth is the mystery of heaven and earth, the mystery of the universe. What is this mystery? This mystery is simply God Himself.

Romans 1:20 says, "For the invisible things of Him, both His eternal power and divine characteristics, have been clearly seen since the creation of the world, being perceived by the things made, so that they would be without excuse." When you see the heaven, the earth, the stars, the sun, and the moon, you cannot deny that there is a sovereign Lord in the universe. Regardless of what you call Him, there is such a One. The entire universe declares the eternal power of God.

In addition to God's eternal power, this verse also refers to a deeper aspect of God, that is, His divine characteristics. The Greek word for *divine characteristics* is a word that is difficult to translate not only in Chinese but also in English. Colossians 2:9 says, "For in Him dwells all the fullness of the Godhead bodily." In Greek, the word for *Godhead* in this verse and the word for *divine characteristics* in Romans 1:20 are of the same root, but they are two entirely different words. The King James Version renders both words as *Godhead*.

Romans 1:20, however, refers to the special features, the characteristics, as the outward manifestations of God's nature. Hence, in this verse we render the Greek word as *divine characteristics*. Colossians 2:9 refers to the divine Godhead, the divine Person, God Himself.

Glory

What then are the divine characteristics as the outward manifestations of the divine nature? Psalm 19:1 says, "The heavens declare the glory of God, / And the firmament proclaims the work of His hands." Here, the glory of God is no doubt manifested by the glory of the sun, the moon, and the stars. The glory of light is a manifestation of the divine characteristics of God's nature. The heavens declare the divine characteristics of God's nature through this particular manifestation. Psalm 8:1-3 says, "O Jehovah...who have set Your glory over the heavens!...When I see...the moon and the stars...." *Glory* here is manifested by the brilliance of the moon and the stars. From these verses we can see that the glory manifested in the universe tells us that the special features, the characteristics, of the divine nature are glorious.

Power and Ability

The work of His hands refers to God's ability, wisdom, and capability. In other words, the universe is God's masterpiece. We may well translate *the work of His hands* into *masterpiece*. In this masterpiece there are wisdom, skillfulness, ability, and power, all of which are characteristics as the outward manifestations of God's nature.

Grandness and Majesty

Furthermore, when you see the universe, you are reminded of God as One who is grand and majestic. Grandness and majesty are also characteristics as manifestations of God's nature.

Light and Life

Moreover, the universe is full of light and life. By this you can see that God's nature is full of light and life. The earth created by God is full of life. There are plants, animals, and humans, all of which are life and are according to the order of life.

God first created the lifeless things, and then He created a lower form of life, the plant life without consciousness. Following this, He created the animal life with consciousness. The life with consciousness begins with the oviparous, the life that is produced by laying eggs, and advances to the viviparous, the life that is brought forth apart from laying eggs. With the viviparous, there are also different levels. Beasts and cattle are viviparous, but they are different in level and size. The highest life of the viviparous variety is man's life. Most people today consider men as animals. We do not agree with that. I am not an animal; I am a man. First, I have God's image, and second, I have a spirit within me. The Chinese also say that man is the "spirit of all creatures." Man is not an animal; man is a life with the image of God.

Finally, the highest life is God's life, signified by the tree of life in Genesis 2. The record in Genesis 1 and 2 begins with the lowest level of life, then it goes up level by level until it reaches the life of man. From there it goes up from the life of man to the life of God, which is the highest life. Praise the Lord, as the regenerated ones we have God's life! When you look at the flowers, grass, trees, insects, fish, birds, beasts, and then the human race, everywhere you look is full of life. This declares to us that life is a divine characteristic of the Creator.

Beauty

Another characteristic of the divine attributes is beauty.

The universe created by God is truly beautiful. Only a God of beauty can create a beautiful universe. Suppose your lawn were not green but black. You would see blackness when you go into your yard, and you would see blackness when you step out of your house. Would you consider that beautiful? Would you like to have such a lawn? The most beautiful thing is to have green trees, green grass, and red flowers. How beautiful, how pleasant to the eyes, and how refreshing are the scenes we see today!

Orderliness

Furthermore, everything in the universe is orderly. Today's scientific research tries to discover the laws and principles in the universe. Since there are laws and principles, there must be one who makes them. If there are laws in a country, there must be a legislature or congress. How could there be laws without lawmakers? How could there be laws and principles in the universe unless it is God who has set them? The moon, the sun, the earth, and the stars revolve within their orbits without colliding. If the earth were a little closer to the sun, we would be burned; if it were a little farther from the sun, we would be frozen. Who defines these things? Who causes the universe to be so orderly, without any confusion? All these things speak forth God's masterpiece and declare God's invisible, eternal power and divine attributes.

GOD AS A DIVINE PERSON

Man can perceive the invisible things of God by observing the visible things created by Him. Both the eternal power of God and the divine characteristics that express God's intrinsic nature are manifested in God's creation. However, this is still not God Himself as a divine Person. What is referred to in Colossians 2:9 is the Godhead, God's person. The characteristics of God's nature, referred to in Romans 1:20, can be verified through the created things; however, the created things cannot manifest the Godhead and person. Only the living person of Jesus Christ, the Word who is God and who declares God (John 1:1, 18), can express God's Godhead and person, that is, the very God, God Himself.

What the Lord Jesus Christ reveals is much deeper than what the universe verifies. What is verified by the universe is only the outward manifestation of God's nature, not His Godhead. Only what is revealed and declared by the living person of the Lord Jesus Christ is God's Godhead and person, that is, the very God Himself. Before we were saved, we could see the characteristics of God's nature manifested through the universe, so that we were without excuse. After we have believed in the Lord Jesus, it is in Christ that we know the divine Godhead. The divine characteristics, which are outward, are manifested through the created things; the divine Godhead, which is God Himself, is lived out through the person of the Lord Jesus Christ.

GOD UPHOLDING AND BEARING ALL THINGS

There are countless items in the universe. In such a boundless and mysterious universe, who is maintaining, managing, upholding, and propelling it? Hebrews 1:3 says, "Who...upholding and bearing all things by the word of His power." The Lord Jesus upholds, bears, and propels all things not by His work but by His instant word, the word of His power. In creation all things came into being through Him as the Word (John 1:1-3). The universe has been framed by the word of God (Heb. 11:3): "For He spoke, and it was; / He commanded, and it stood" (Psa. 33:9). God speaks and upholds all things with His word. According to Greek grammar, this upholding is continuous, unceasing. The Greek word for *upholding* implies several rich meanings, including maintaining, operating, managing, controlling, and even propelling.

The Lord Jesus as the Mighty God maintains, operates, manages, controls, and propels all things. He not only upholds all things for their mere existence but also maintains and propels them. This may be compared to a huge airplane. Once the engines are started, the airplane is upheld and maintained in the sky. Today no one can deny that the mystery of the universe is with God. God is the meaning and center of the universe; He is the purpose of the universe.

Without God, the entire universe is empty and dead. The meaning of the universe is the living God. As the living Spirit,

He is omnipresent, and He is also a divine Person. You need only to open your heart and pray to Him, and He will enter into you. Then you will become a person with meaning, and you will enjoy God as the mystery of the entire universe.

CHAPTER TWO

THE MYSTERY OF MAN

Scripture Reading: Gen. 1:27; Zech. 12:1; Rom. 9:21-23; John
4:24; 3:5, 14-15; Gen. 2:7

In the previous chapter we saw that in the Bible there are
the five great mysteries: the universe, man, God, Christ, and
the church. Apart from these five great mysteries, there are
many other mysteries in the Bible. The Gospel of Matthew
speaks of the mysteries of the kingdom. The Gospel of John
and the first Epistle of John also contain many mysteries,
such as the mystery of eternal life and the mystery of God
becoming flesh. The other books of the New Testament also
speak of the mystery of our rapture, the mystery of resurrection, and others.

Eternal life is a mystery. Eternal life is not a matter of
blessing but a matter of life. The Greek word for *eternal*
applies not only to time but also to sphere; it implies time and
extent. With respect to time, this life is everlasting; with
respect to extent, this life is unlimited. Hence, this life is the
eternal life. Such a life is mysterious to us. The fellowship
produced out of this life is also mysterious.

In Greek the word for *mystery* implies "the shutting of the
mouth," "being silenced." Suppose this morning as an old Chinese man I come and stand here silent with my mouth shut.
You sit in silence for ninety minutes, and I stand also in
silence for ninety minutes. As a result, you all will say, "This
is really a mystery! We went to the meeting this morning, but
we did not hear anything. We only saw a mysterious situation. The preacher simply would not tell us what was hidden
inside his being. What a mystery!"

The universe is a mystery; the universe is mysterious.

This means that God kept His mouth shut. God created the heavens and the earth; then He created all things in great variety; and eventually He created man. To not have the Holy Bible would mean that God has kept silent. Thus, everything in the universe would be a mystery, and we would not be able to understand anything or know anything at all.

GOD'S COMING BRINGING REVELATION

The way the Chinese sages formed Chinese words is truly interesting. The Chinese word for *God* is made up of two characters: the one on the left means to reveal, and the one on the right means to explain. God is the One who has revealed Himself and who has spoken. When you do not have God, everything is a mystery, but when God comes, revelation comes; then you have light and you are clear. One day before I turned nineteen, I heard the pure gospel and received it. I remember very clearly that on the afternoon I received God, immediately there was brightness within me. This was revelation; this was God coming into me. Dear brothers and sisters, how do you know if you have God in you? God is in you because there is brightness in you, and there is revelation in you.

What is revelation? Revelation is the opening of the veil to reveal the hidden things. The subject of the book of Revelation is the "opening of the veil." The book of Revelation fully reveals how in the universe there is God's dominion in heaven and how there is God Himself on earth; it also reveals how God reigns in heaven and on earth and how the Lord is the center of the reigning in the universe. Today, we are not under God's silence. God's mystery which has been kept in silence in the times of the ages has now been manifested through the prophetic writings according to the command of the eternal God (Rom. 16:25-26).

Today, we have an open Bible, and the entire Bible is God's revelation. Hebrews 1 begins by saying, "God, having spoken of old in many portions and in many ways to the fathers in the prophets, has at the last of these days spoken to us in the Son." In the Old Testament, God spoke in the prophets, in men borne by His Spirit. In the New Testament, God speaks in the Son, that is, in the person of the Son.

THE MYSTERY OF MAN

Now let us come to see the second great mystery in the Bible, which is the mystery of man. Actually, the mystery of man is the mystery of you. All the abstract, invisible, spiritual, living things are surely mysterious, but our human body is also mysterious. Our eyes are more complex than the most advanced cameras today. Even the hairs of our body are mysteries. All the hairs in our body grow downward; only the hairs in our trachea grow upward. Some up and some down: what a mystery! This mystery is very logical. If the hairs on our body were to grow upward, it would be inconvenient for us to take a bath or shower. But if the hairs in our trachea were to grow downward, we would be in trouble, because all the dirty things would go down and accumulate in the lungs; we would not even be able to cough out phlegm. Is this not marvelous?

The first mystery in the Bible is the universe, and the mystery of the universe is God. Man also is a mystery, and the mystery of man is God. We must ask ourselves: Do we have God? How much do we enjoy God? Just to have the name and understand the theory are not enough. You must enjoy God in reality as the meaning of your human life.

MAN BEING ACCORDING TO GOD'S KIND

The Bible shows us that God's creation of heaven, earth, and all things was from the lowest to the highest, with man being created last. Furthermore, all the living creatures that God created were each according to its kind. The fish was according to the fish kind, and the bird was according to the bird kind; so then man must be according to mankind. But according to the revelation in the Bible, man is neither of the animal kind nor according to mankind. Man is superior and is different from the insects, fish, birds, and beasts. Man is of the same kind as God because man was created according to the image of God. Like a photograph of God, man bears the appearance of God. But even though man was created according to God's kind and bears the image of God, he did not have the life of God.

Genesis 1:26 says, "And God said, Let Us make man in Our image, according to Our likeness." The *Us* here refers to the Triune God—the Father, the Son, and the Spirit. The Father, the Son, and the Spirit wanted to create man in Their image and after Their likeness. But when we reach verse 27, it says, "And God created man in His own image; in the image of God He created him; male and female He created them." The pronoun *Us* in verse 26 becomes a singular pronoun *He*. It is clearly *Us* in one verse, yet the next verse says *He*. Why is this? If you continue to read the Bible, you will find the answer when you reach the New Testament. Actually, Jesus Christ is the image of God (Col. 1:15); He is the effulgence of God's glory and the impress of God's substance (Heb. 1:3). Hence, God's creation of man in the beginning was according to Christ.

Christ may be likened to the molding pan used by women for making bread. The molding pans used by the northern Chinese have seven different shapes: a dog, a tiger, a rabbit, a bird, a persimmon, a peach, and an apple. If you put the dough into the molds, you can make snacks of different shapes. Christ is the mold, and we are the clay. God created man with Christ as the mold. Therefore, man had the image of Christ, but he did not have the life of Christ. Why did God create man in this way? It was for the purpose that one day He could put Christ into man. This may be compared to making gloves. All the pairs of gloves are made for the purpose that one day men could put their hands into the gloves. Christ is the content of man as a glove. If you do not have Christ within you, then you are an empty glove; you are deflated. When you receive the Lord Jesus as your Savior, He enters into you. Then you are no longer an empty glove, but you are filled and satisfied. Man was created according to Christ and for Christ, just as a glove is made according to the hand and for the hand. Without the hand, the glove is meaningless and empty. Without Christ, man is empty and unsatisfied. In creation, man had only the image of Christ but not the life of Christ.

GOD USING DUST AND THE BREATH OF LIFE
TO CREATE MAN

In Genesis 2 we are told what kinds of material God used to create man and how He created man. First, God used the dust of the ground to create man's body. It is unmistakable that man's body is of the ground. Genesis 3:19 says that man was taken out of the ground and that man is dust and will return to dust. However, God breathed the breath of life into man's nostrils, into his body, and man became a living soul with a spirit (Gen. 2:7). There were two kinds of material used: one was dust, which is concrete and visible; the other was breath, which is abstract and invisible. The dust was used to form man's body, and the breath was breathed into man to become man's spirit.

Here we see two kinds of material: dust and breath. The dust formed man's body, and the breath became man's spirit. The combination of the two produces the soul. This is why the Bible says that man is a living soul. In the Bible the soul is the unit for counting people. Seventy people of Jacob's household went down into Egypt, but the Bible says seventy souls went down into Egypt (Gen. 46:27, KJV).

In the Hebrew language, the word for *breath* in "the breath of life" in Genesis 2:7 is the same word for *spirit* in "The spirit of man is the lamp of Jehovah" in Proverbs 20:27. This proves that the breath of life that God breathed into man entered into man to become his spirit. Proverbs 20:27 says that the spirit of man is the lamp of Jehovah. This means that man's spirit is the lamp to contain Jehovah as the oil for the lamp to shine. Therefore, if the spirit within man does not have God, it becomes a useless lamp. The spirit within us is a lamp, and it needs God to come into it as oil for us to be lit and to shine forth.

This becomes clearer in the New Testament. Today, when we believe in the Lord and receive Him into us, this God who is oil enters into us and dwells in our spirit. The parable of the ten virgins in Matthew 25 shows us that the five prudent virgins had oil in their vessels, but the five foolish virgins did not have oil in their vessels. This means that some Christians do not have sufficient oil within. This may be compared to driving your car to the meeting; if you do not have enough gas, it should not be a surprise to you when your car stops halfway. Today, many Christians are Christians with insufficient oil, Christians who have "stopped halfway." The surest way is for us to first go to the house of God to get oil every day. We need to read the Bible and pray every day. We should first go to the "gas station" and get a full tank of gas before we start driving. We need to do this every morning to ensure that we will never be short of gas and stop short. Thank the Lord that God created a spirit for us! This spirit within us is the lamp of Jehovah God, and God is the oil within the lamp.

THE SOUL BEING CORRUPTED IN MAN'S FALL

When God created man, the soul was originally good. One school of Chinese philosophy advocates that man's nature is good by birth, while another school maintains that man's nature is evil by birth. Actually, both are correct. When man was first created, man's nature (referring to man's soul) was good. When Satan came in to damage man, man fell and was united with Satan; thus, man's nature became evil. Therefore, when the Chinese sages were forming word characters, due to man's fallen condition they included the word *demon* as part of the word for *soul*. The word for *soul* is made up of *demon* and *speaking;* hence, the soul is the demon speaking. This is true especially when a man is angry and loses his temper; the more he speaks, the more he becomes a "demon."

Man's soul became fallen and was united with Satan. This is why the Lord Jesus said, "If anyone wants to come after Me, let him deny himself and take up his cross and follow Me" (Matt. 16:24). To deny our self is to lose our soul-life, our natural life. Our attitude as Christians should be to never follow our soul, to always exercise to deny our self, and to take up the cross to follow the Lord.

Man was created in God's image and after God's likeness with a spirit, a soul, and a body for the purpose of containing God. However, the created life of man was not the life of God, and the spirit of man was not the Spirit of God but something that issued from God's breath of life. Some Bible scholars say that the breath of God in Genesis 2:7 refers to the life of God.

This is wrong, because after God created man, He placed man in front of the tree of life, which signifies God Himself. God's intention was for man to receive the tree of life, which was to receive God Himself, but man fell, and Satan entered in. Therefore, God closed the way to the tree of life so that man had no way to approach the tree of life and receive God as life.

Then a time came when God Himself became flesh to satisfy God's righteousness, meet God's holiness, and express God's glory. He declared that He was life, that He was that tree. Moreover, He told us that He came that man may have life and may have it abundantly. Finally, He died on the cross and opened a new and living way for us, so that we who were alienated from God, signified by the tree of life, can enter into the Holy of Holies to contact Him and take Him as the tree of life for our enjoyment.

TAKING CARE OF OUR SPIRIT

Today, our spirit is the most important part of our entire being. The human spirit is the organ for receiving God as life. We are just like a radio. A radio has a receiver within it. When the receiver malfunctions, it cannot receive the radio waves. Man is like a radio, and the human spirit within him is like a receiver. However, due to man's fall, very few people take care of the spirit within. Man cares only for the outward body and the soul. When we repented and were saved, our spirit was activated. In other words, our conscience was activated.

According to the record in the Bible, the conscience is the leading part of the spirit. The conscience is the "bright virtue" taught by Confucius and the "inherent goodness" or "the brightness of the human heart" taught by Wang Yang-ming. Now that you are saved, you need to take care of your spirit. In the past when you quarreled with your wife, you were never short of words to defend yourself, and the more you spoke, the more you were convinced that you were right. But after you heard the gospel, the Holy Spirit entered into you and touched your conscience, causing your spirit and conscience to function. Then you confessed your sins and repented. The more you confessed, the stronger the spirit became. The more you confessed your sins, the clearer and purer your spirit became. This means that God came in, the oil came into the lamp, and the lamp was lit. When you have light and revelation, that means God has come into you. However, after many of us have been saved, we put aside our lamp and do not care for the spirit. We are accustomed to using our mentality, our mind, but not our spirit. Although we know that as believers we should turn to our spirit and care for our spirit, yet we seldom do so.

LIVING IN SPIRIT TO BE A VESSEL OF GOD

Zechariah 12:1 says, "Jehovah, who stretches forth the heavens and lays the foundations of the earth and forms the spirit of man within him." In God's eyes, man is of equal importance with heaven and earth. Moreover, heaven and earth are for man; so man is the center. Without the earth, man could not live. Without heaven, the earth would be without rain and sunlight and thus would not be able to sustain all the living things. The animals could not live; the plants could not live; and even more, man could not live. The vast heaven is for the earth, and the earth is for man. Although heaven is great, it is for the earth; although the earth is big, it is for the small man; and although man is small, he is for God. God is Spirit, and the man who is for God must also have a spirit so that the two spirits can become one spirit. It is no wonder that the Chinese sages said that man is the "spirit of all things." The heaven is for the earth, and the earth is for man and for the spirit within man, so that man could live in his spirit to be God's vessel to receive, contain, express, and manifest God for God's satisfaction.

Today, we Christians have God within us. We are not here merely to eat but to contain God, to express God, and to be God's vessels. The Chinese have a saying, "Man's life is a matter of three fillings and one falling." *Three fillings* are the eating of three meals, whereas *one falling* refers to sleeping. Our Christian life is not for "three fillings and one falling." We were created by God as a tripartite man with a spirit, a soul, and a body for us to contain, enjoy, and express God.

Perhaps you have not yet believed in the Lord. In this

case, you must know that you are a vessel created for God. God wants you to be a vessel unto honor and glory to contain Him. Because God wants you to contain Him, He created a precious spirit in you. This spirit is for containing God. If you do not have God as Spirit in your spirit, your human life is vanity. If you have God as Spirit in you, your human life is substantial. If a radio is never turned on but is always laid aside, even though it has a receiver, it is still vanity. If it is laid aside for a day, it will be vanity for a day; if it is laid aside for a lifetime, it will be empty for a lifetime. You simply need to open your heart to the Lord to receive Him by calling on His name. Do not stay in your mind. You have a spirit within you. You must let your spirit function and let the conscience in your spirit function by speaking to you. You must follow the sense of your conscience and confess your sins to God. God will surely forgive your sins and even enter into you, and you will then be regenerated. When God comes in, the heavenly "music" also comes in. When God comes in, revelation comes in, light comes in, and life comes in.

Today, we should not use our mind to worship God; rather, we need to use our spirit to worship. Only that which is born of the Spirit is spirit. Only the Spirit can beget the spirit; only the spirit can worship the Spirit. I hope that these words could unravel the mystery of man. Man is a mystery because he has a spirit in him that enables him to let God come in to be his life and meaning. Thus, God becomes the mystery of man. Thank and praise the Lord! God is not only the mystery and meaning of the universe; even more He is the mystery and meaning of man.

CHAPTER THREE

THE MYSTERY OF GOD

Scripture Reading: Col. 2:2, 9; 3:4, 10-11; John 1:18, 16; Heb. 1:3

In this chapter we want to see the third great mystery in the Bible. This mystery, which is the mystery of mysteries and the center of all the mysteries, is the mystery of God. The mystery of the universe and the mystery of man in reality are just one. The mystery of the universe is God, and the mystery of man is also God. In a general sense, God is the mystery of the universe; in a particular sense, God is the mystery of man. God is the mystery of the universe and of man. Furthermore, God Himself is a mystery. This mystery is simply Christ.

THE MYSTERY OF GOD BEING CHRIST

This is the mystery of God preached by the apostle Paul (1 Cor. 2:1). This is not the shallow revelation that so many have preached; it is the mystery hidden in the depths of God. This mystery is not any superficial aspect of the gospel; it is the intrinsic reality of the complete gospel of God. This reality is Christ as the mystery of God.

If we want to know how Christ is the mystery of God, we need to study the first two chapters of Colossians. Colossians 1 and 2 tell us what kind of person Christ is.

CHRIST AS THE PORTION OF THE SAINTS

Colossians 1:12 says that Christ is the God-allotted portion of the saints. In the Old Testament, God allotted the land of Canaan, the land flowing with milk and honey, to the tribes of Israel; each tribe received a portion. This portion became the inheritance and blessing of the children of Israel. Today, in the New Testament, Christ is our God-given portion as our inheritance. This portion, this inheritance, is the spiritual blessing which we have received.

CHRIST AS THE IMAGE OF GOD

Colossians 1:15 says that Christ, who is the Son of God's love, is the image of the invisible God. The image here is not a physical image but an expression of all that God is. Christ as the Son of God's love has God's life and nature, so John 1:18 and 14:7-9 say that He expresses the Father. Because He expresses the Father, He is the image of the invisible God. God is invisible, but the Son of God's love, having God's life and nature, can express God; therefore, He is the image of God. This is the relationship between Christ and God.

CHRIST AS THE FIRSTBORN OF ALL CREATION

Colossians 1:15 goes on to say that Christ is "the Firstborn of all creation." Christ is the first One among all creatures. This speaks of Christ having the preeminence among all creatures. With regard to Christ being God, He is the Creator; but with regard to Christ being man, He is a creature. Since He became a man and partook of the created blood and flesh, to be sure He is part of creation. Among the creatures, after the first Adam fell, there was a last Adam. If Christ was not a creature, how could He become the last Adam? If He was not a creature, He could not have become the last Adam. Adam is the name of a created one. You cannot say that the first Adam was created, yet the last Adam was not. To say this is not logical.

According to the original text of Colossians 1:15, we cannot deny that in God's creation, Christ is the first created One, who has preeminence in all creation. If He was not the first created One, He could not have the first place in all creation. For Him to have the first place among all creatures, He needed to become the first created One. Praise the Lord that He is not only the Creator but also a creature! Furthermore, He is the first of all creation because He wants to have the first place in all creation. He was a created man so He could die and shed blood for us. If He was not a creature but was only God the Creator, He could not have died, because God can never die. Some people say, "Our Christ is only the Creator." In this case, I want to ask, "Does the Creator have blood? Does the almighty Creator have flesh and blood? If He had no blood, how could He shed blood for us?" (Acts 20:28).

Dear brothers and sisters, we should not be deceived. Of course, our Lord is the Creator. However, He is also a creature. This is why He is all-inclusive. Because He is a creature, He could die. He actually died by being crucified. Furthermore, He was buried in a tomb. If He was only the Creator and not a creature, would it not be absurd for Him to be buried in a tomb?

Thank and praise the Lord that He also resurrected! In His resurrection, His physical body was transformed into a spiritual body. First Corinthians 15 clearly says that through such a resurrection, He as the last Adam became the life-giving Spirit. Although He is the life-giving Spirit, He still has humanity. When He went back to the disciples after His resurrection, He went with a resurrected body. He showed them His hands and His side, and He told them to touch His side and the nail marks on His hands (John 20:19-27). He is indeed the Spirit, but He still has a human body, so surely He has humanity. Therefore, today He is still the Son of Man in heaven (Acts 7:56); in His coming back He will still be the Son of Man (Matt. 25:31); and even in eternity He will also be the Son of Man for eternity (John 1:51).

CHRIST AS THE CREATOR
AND THE ONE IN WHOM ALL THINGS COHERE

Colossians 1:16 tells us that Christ is the Creator of all things. All things in the heavens and on the earth, the visible and the invisible, whether thrones or lordships or rulers or authorities, were created in the power of Christ's person, in the power of what Christ is. All creation bears the characteristics of Christ's intrinsic power. All these have been created through Him, for Him, and unto Him.

Furthermore, verse 17 tells us that "He is before all things, and all things cohere in Him." Christ is not only the Creator of all things but also the One in whom all things cohere. He is the cohering center of all things. All things exist together by Christ as the holding center, just as the spokes of a wheel are held together by the hub at their center. Verses 15b to 17 speak of the relationship between Christ and the old creation.

CHRIST AS THE HEAD OF THE CHURCH, THE BODY, AS THE BEGINNING, AND AS THE FIRSTBORN FROM THE DEAD

Verse 18 tells us that Christ is the Head of the Body, the church; He is the beginning, the Firstborn from the dead. This means that in resurrection Christ has the first place in the new creation, the church. He is the Head of the Body, the beginning, and the Firstborn from the dead, the first to be resurrected from the dead to have the preeminence in the church. This shows us His relationship with the new creation.

God has two great creations in the universe: one is the old creation and the other is the new creation. In the old creation, Christ is the Firstborn of all creation that He might have the first place in the old creation. In the new creation, Christ is the first to be resurrected that He might have the first place in the new creation. Because He has the first place in both the old creation and in the new creation, being the first in all creation, He has the preeminence in all things in the universe. This is because it pleased God to have all the fullness dwell in Him (v. 19).

CHRIST AS THE REDEEMER TO US AND TO ALL THINGS

Colossians 1:20-22 tells us that on the cross Christ accomplished redemption for us and all things. He made peace through the precious blood which He shed on the cross to reconcile us and all things, whether the things on the earth or the things in the heavens, to God. Not only did we need God's redemption, but due to the fall of Adam as their head, all things also needed God's redemption. Through His death and the shedding of His blood once for all, the all-inclusive Christ accomplished the full salvation which we and all things needed. This shows us the relationship of Christ to God's redemption.

CHRIST AS THE HOPE OF GLORY IN THE BELIEVERS

Verse 27 tells us that Christ has become the hope of glory in us, the believers. Today, Christ within us is our life and everything; He is also our hope for the future. He is within us as life that we may have a hope, which is the redemption of our body for our whole being to enter into His glory (Rom. 8:21, 23; Phil. 3:21). This speaks of the relationship of Christ with His believers.

Then Colossians 2:2 tells us that such a Christ is the mystery of God. This means that, as God's story and God's everything, Christ declares God in full. Verse 3 says that all the treasures of wisdom and knowledge are hidden in Him. The mention of wisdom and knowledge here has its background. According to history, the influence of Gnostic teaching, which included Greek philosophy, had invaded the Gentile churches in Paul's time. Those who were influenced by such teaching considered themselves as having much wisdom and knowledge.•They spoke many things concerning God and Christ that were not according to the truth. Hence, Paul told the Colossian believers that all the treasures of genuine wisdom and knowledge are hidden in Christ. Here, wisdom and knowledge refer to all the "stories" of God. All the stories of God are wisdom and knowledge. All the wisdom and knowledge pertaining to God's stories are hidden in this Christ who is the mystery of God. This being the case, Colossians 2:6-7 tells us that we who have received Christ Jesus the Lord should walk in Him and be rooted and built up in Him and should not listen to the empty words of philosophy and philosophical doctrines of the Gnostics.

CHRIST AS ALL THE FULLNESS OF THE GODHEAD

Colossians 2:9 says, "For in Him dwells all the fullness of the Godhead bodily." This is a very great verse in the Bible. All the words used here, such as *all, fullness,* and *Godhead,* are very special. The Greek word for *Godhead* is *theotes,* which is very similar to the Greek word *theiotes* used in Romans 1:20 for *divine characteristics* with only a one-letter difference. Both are derived from the same Greek word.

Therefore, the King James Version translates both words as *Godhead*. *Theiotes* denotes the divine characteristics manifested through the created things, while *theotes* denotes the deity of Christ. I have used wood grain as an illustration. The meeting hall in Irving, Texas was built with oak, which is a unique product of Texas. The Texan oak has a very striking grain. It is a distinctive feature of the Texan oak, or we may say, it is a characteristic of the nature of the Texan oak.

Characteristics are always manifested. In contrast, substance is not manifested. *Substance* is a stronger word than *nature* because substance has not only the nature of a certain thing but also the very essence of that thing. "All the fullness of the Godhead" is "all the fullness of God's essence." Here it is not speaking about God's intrinsic nature or divine characteristics but the very substance of God. God's substance is simply God Himself, so we can translate it as *Godhead*. *Godhead* refers to God Himself.

Colossians 2:9 says that all the fullness of the very substance of God dwells in Christ bodily. Christ is truly not so simple; all the fullness of God's very substance dwells in Him bodily. He is all-inclusive and comprehensive. The Son of God's love, the image of God, the Firstborn of all creation, the Firstborn from the dead, the Redeemer, and the Godhead all are not simple, not to mention the mystery of God. All the fullness of God's substance dwells in Christ bodily. Hence, Christ is the mystery of God, the story of God.

CHRIST AS GOD AND MAN

Christ is God who became flesh to become a man. His Godhead and divinity are complete, and His person and humanity are also genuine. The title *Christ* means the anointed One (Dan. 9:26). Christ was anointed by God (Luke 4:18) to be God's anointed One to accomplish God's redemption and fulfill God's eternal plan. God's eternal plan is for man to be His expression. This requires God to work Himself into man to become man's life, to be united with him, and to live Himself out from within man. However, because the man who was created for God's plan fell, God Himself needed to become a man to die and bear the sins for man that He might redeem man back to be God's vessel, so that God can live in man and be his content and express Himself from within man. Christ was anointed by God for the very purpose of carrying out this plan of God. This is the great, divine commission. This great, divine commission requires Christ to have the dual status of God and man, fully equipped with the divine nature and power and the human nature and character. Hence, Christ needed to be both God and man, to be completely God and genuinely man.

As God, Christ had the divine life and nature and was able to dispense God in His life and nature to man, enabling man to live out God's attributes to express and glorify God. As God, Christ also possessed the unlimited power of God to do the unlimited work of God and to make all His work unlimitedly effective.

As man, Christ had the human life and nature so that He was the same as man in life and nature. Christ was like man in all respects, except that He was without sin. This enabled Him to sympathize with man and save man (Heb. 2:17; 4:15). Christ as a man with human flesh and blood suffered death through crucifixion, shedding human blood to make redemption for man's sins. Because of the guarantee of the unlimited power of His divinity, the redemption which Christ accomplished in His human nature and human body had an eternal, unlimited effect, thereby becoming an eternal redemption (9:12). By His resurrection from the dead, the human nature and human body of Christ were uplifted through union with His divine life and nature. His humanity was brought into His divinity, and His human body became a spiritual body (1 Cor. 15:44). Thus, Christ became the Redeemer who redeemed us from sin and the Savior who dispensed life into us. Thank and praise Him! Christ is both God and man; He is the God-man who has become such a complete and wonderful Redeemer and Savior.

CHRIST HAVING BECOME THE LIFE-GIVING SPIRIT

In order to accomplish God's eternal redemption and plan, Christ as God's Anointed took two great steps. First, as God He was incarnated to become a man (John 1:1, 14), the last

Adam (1 Cor. 15:45b), that He might die and accomplish redemption for us (Heb. 9:26-28; 10:12). Second, through death and resurrection He as the last Adam became a life-giving Spirit (1 Cor. 15:45b) that He may enter into us (John 14:20) to be our life (Col. 3:4) and to live in us (Gal. 2:20) that we may live Him out (Phil. 1:20-21).

By these two great steps Christ passed through incarnation and tasted all the sufferings of human life; then He died and was resurrected. From being God He became a man, and from being a man He became the Spirit. Thus He accomplished God's eternal redemption and full salvation to carry out the commission for which He was anointed by God.

CHRIST BEING ALL-INCLUSIVE

In resurrection Christ became the life-giving Spirit, who is the Spirit indwelling us today (Rom. 8:9-11). This indwelling Spirit is all-inclusive. The incarnated Christ is in this Spirit; the resurrected Christ is in this Spirit; even all of the Triune God is in this Spirit for us to experience. This life-giving Spirit as everything and as the reality of Christ is in us to be our life and all our supply within.

In 1966, I wrote many hymns in Taiwan, one of which was *Hymns,* #510: "I've found the One of peerless worth, / My heart doth sing for joy; / And sing I must, for Christ I have: / Oh, what a Christ have I!" In this hymn, I pointed out over thirty items of what Christ is. Our Christ is all-inclusive! The last part of this hymn says, "My Christ, the all-inclusive One, / My Christ what shall I call? / He is the first, He is the last, / My Christ is All in all." This is our Christ, who is the mystery of God.

CHRIST AS GOD'S FULLNESS AND GOD'S EXPRESSION

Romans 1:20 says that through the created things we can know the invisible things of God, both His eternal power and divine characteristics. The divine characteristics include glory, truth, wisdom, light, love, and others. Through all the created things, man is able to know all these manifested characteristics of God. However, the very substance of God Himself cannot be expressed by the created things. Only a living / Person—Jesus Christ—can fully express it. Therefore, if we want to know the substance of God, we must know Christ. God's substance, which is all the fullness of the Godhead, dwells in Christ bodily (Col. 2:9). Christ is the embodiment of God. Hence, Hebrews 1:3 says that Christ is the "effulgence of His glory and the impress of His substance."

What the created things express are only the outward manifested characteristics of God, not God's intrinsic substance or God's own being. The mysterious substance of God, the glorious deity of God, could be expressed perfectly only by the incarnated Christ. When Christ was living on the earth, all His move and work showed people God Himself, God's substance. This is why John 1:18 says, "No one has ever seen God; the only begotten Son, who is in the bosom of the Father, He has declared Him." This only begotten Son who declared the Father is God's embodiment. Hence, His disciples called Him God.

What Christ expressed was the overflow of the fullness of the Godhead which was in Him. John 1:16 says, "For of His fullness we have all received." This is not only riches, but even more this is fullness, being so full to the extent of overflowing to become an expression. Our Lord was so full of God's substance within that He overflowed God's substance to become God's expression. Hence, He is God's fullness and God's expression.

CHRIST AS OUR LIFE

Colossians 3:4 goes a step further to tell us that this all-inclusive Christ, who is God's expression, is our life. This is not objective but subjective. It is something within us. Now this Christ is sitting at the right hand of God (3:1) in the heavens, but He is also within us as our life and everything. This is truly too mysterious and too glorious! This life is the life of God, including all the riches of God. When we live by this life, we enjoy everything of God!

CHRIST AS EVERYTHING
TO THE NEW MAN, THE CHURCH

Following this, 3:10-11 tells us that this all-inclusive

Christ who is life within us makes us a corporate new man. This new man is composed of all the saints who have Him as life. The content of this new man is not our natural man: not Scythian nor Jew nor Chinese nor American nor German nor Japanese nor Filipino nor Malaysian. The content of this new man is Christ, who is the mystery of God and who is the life in all men. He is the life of the new man, and He is everything to the new man.

CHAPTER FOUR

THE MYSTERY OF CHRIST

Scripture Reading: Eph. 3:4; Col. 1:27; Eph. 3:6; Rom. 12:5; 1 Cor. 12:12; Eph. 1:23

In this chapter we want to see the fourth great mystery in the Bible—the mystery of Christ. However, before we fellowship about the mystery of Christ, I feel that I have the responsibility to fellowship in detail with you the truth concerning the person of Christ. It is only when we see this truth that we can enter into the subjective experience of Christ and live out the mystery of Christ, which is the church. This truth is neglected by Christianity today. The mystery of Christ is the church; the content and expression of Christ are the church. If we have only the objective knowledge but not the subjective experience of Christ, this mystery will become an empty doctrine. Dear brothers and sisters, we cannot be deceived. We must know the truth. In order to fellowship about this truth, I cannot avoid referring to certain things in our "family history" which can serve as a background and provide a contrast to this truth.

"THOU, LORD, THE FATHER ONCE WAST CALLED, BUT NOW THE HOLY SPIRIT ART"

I started to correspond with Brother Nee in 1925. In 1932, Brother Nee went to my hometown to hold a special conference, and we started to have face-to-face contact. In the following year, I left my work, and he wrote me a letter which confirmed my leaving my job to serve the Lord full time. Hence, after I left my job, I went to Shanghai particularly to see him. In the beginning of 1933, we began to work together until the political situation in mainland China changed in

1949. At that time, he called an emergency co-workers' meeting to decide on how to cope with the changes. Two times in the co-workers' meetings he suggested that I leave mainland China and go overseas. Therefore, in April or May of 1949 I went to Taiwan. The following year Brother Nee went to Hong Kong and brought in a revival. Then he wanted me to go there to arrange all the church services of the co-workers, elders, and deacons. After staying there for one and a half months, I returned to Taiwan. Just before I left for Taiwan, Brother Nee went back to mainland China. In 1952 he was put into prison, and after twenty years of imprisonment he was taken by the Lord in 1972.

I worked with Brother Nee for almost twenty years and had a very close relationship with him in the work. We had much time together. He and I never engaged in any idle talk; we always talked about the truth and the Lord's work. I knew the burden within his heart for the Lord, his view concerning the church, and his way of carrying out the work. Brother Nee absolutely believed that the Triune God is simply Christ Himself. *Hymns,* #490 was written by Brother Nee himself, and two lines of the hymn say, "Thou, Lord, the Father once wast called, / But now the Holy Spirit art." This hymn was first printed in Shanghai and was included in the hymnal with 1,052 selections that Brother Nee had published before he went into prison.

At the end of 1933, a certain Mr. Hsueh, who was a Chinese traveling preacher from the China Inland Mission, was invited to speak in our meeting in Shanghai. He said, "Never think that the Father is the Father, the Son is the Son, and the Spirit is the Spirit, and that the three are separated. Never think that the Lord Jesus is not the Holy Spirit; the Lord Jesus is the Holy Spirit Himself." Brother Nee was sitting at the back listening. When Brother Hsueh mentioned this point, Brother Nee responded far from the back, "Amen!" Even we who were seated in front heard it. After the meeting when he and I were strolling together, he said, "We all must see that the Lord Jesus is the Holy Spirit." Beginning with Brother Nee up until now, the belief among us concerning the

Triune God is that the Father, the Son, and the Spirit are one and not separated.

In 1954 I was invited by the church in Hong Kong to hold a conference. For at least seven days, I spoke with much emphasis on this truth. Every time after I spoke, the brother who accompanied me on the platform prayed to conclude the meeting. His prayer completely confirmed what I spoke. The emphasis of my speaking was that the Triune God had become the indwelling Spirit. I also especially selected some hymns in this category for the congregation to sing. However, after Brother Nee was imprisoned, that brother who had accompanied me changed and said that this was heresy, thereby stirring up contention, which eventually led to division.

"O LORD, THOU ART THE SPIRIT"

In 1963, I began to compile an English hymnal with the help of an American brother, and I wrote a hymn that says, "O Lord, Thou art the Spirit now." I also wrote another hymn that says, "O Lord, Thou art the Spirit! / How dear and near to me." In 1964, I went to New York to lead a conference and training, and this American brother also went. There was a dissenting brother who, upon seeing this American brother polishing these hymns, said to him, "Don't work on these hymns."

After a few days, I sat down to fellowship with this dissenting brother. He said, "The Bible does say that Christ is the Spirit, but today Christianity cannot accept this. If you speak this, you will stir up opposition from Christianity." Then I said, "Brother, my burden today is mainly to speak on Christ as the Spirit. If I do not speak this, I have nothing to speak. I ask that you and the other brothers give me the liberty. If we are afraid of opposition, then what will the Lord's recovery do? When Martin Luther spoke on justification by faith during his time, he was very much opposed by the Catholic Church. Did he stop speaking because he was afraid of people's opposition? If he did not speak, from where would the Reformation have come? Today, the Lord's recovery is still not completed, we cannot stop speaking simply because we are afraid of people's opposition."

THE ETERNAL FATHER
BEING THE REDEEMER FROM OF OLD

Isaiah 9:6 says, "For a child is born to us, / A son is given to us... / And His name will be called / Wonderful Counselor, / Mighty God, / Eternal Father, / Prince of Peace." These two terms—*Mighty God* and *Eternal Father*—are placed next to each other. On the one hand, He is the mighty God; on the other hand, He is the eternal Father. We need to read the subsequent portions in Isaiah for an explanation of the term *Eternal Father*. To interpret every verse of the Bible, we need the entire Bible.

Isaiah 63:16 says, "For You are our Father, / Since Abraham does not know us, / And Israel does not acknowledge us. / You, Jehovah, are our Father; / Our Redeemer from of old is Your name." Here *our Father* and *our Redeemer* are put together. Both our Father and our Redeemer are Jehovah. Jehovah in the Old Testament is Jesus in the New Testament. *Je-* refers to Jehovah, and *-sus,* which was added, means *Savior.* Jehovah becoming the Savior is Jesus. Here it says, "You, Jehovah, are our Father; / Our Redeemer from of old is Your name." This One is Jesus. Here it does not say, "You, God, are our Father" but "You, Jehovah, are our Father." This Father is Jehovah our Savior, who is Jesus. Could it be that Isaiah was telling us about two Fathers: one Father—the eternal Father—in 9:6 and another Father—Jehovah—in 63:16? This is impossible!

Isaiah 64:8 says, "But now, Jehovah, You are our Father." Then 63:16 says, "You, Jehovah, are our Father; / Our Redeemer from of old is Your name." This implies that Jehovah is our Father from of old. Jehovah being our Father from of old equals His being our eternal Father. *From of old* means from eternity, eternally existing. The eternal Father, the Redeemer, from of old, is the One who is our Father from of old. Then 64:8 says, "But now, Jehovah, You are our Father." Jehovah is our Father from of old, and now He is still our Father. According to what is recorded in the entire book of

Isaiah, we can conclude that "Eternal Father" in 9:6 is both Jehovah and Jesus. Hence, 9:6 says that although He is the Son, His name is called *Eternal Father*. This means that He is the Son as well as the Father.

There is a group of opposers near Orange County, California in the United States who studied Isaiah 9:6. In the record of their studies there was a conversation like this: One said, "Isaiah 9:6 surely said that Jesus is the Father!" Another said, "Yes, but we dare not say so. If we say so, then we contradict the traditional teaching." These words were all printed in the booklet we wrote in rebuttal. Up to today, however, at least five or six years have gone by, and they still have not published a book to refute our rebuttal. This is because they have no ground to refute. The truth is the truth.

In Isaiah 9:6 there is another proof that the Son is the eternal Father. This poetic prophecy was written in couplets. In the Hebrew language, couplets are often employed to refer to the same thing. "For a child is born to us, / A son is given to us" is a couplet. Then it goes on to say, "And His name will be called... / Mighty God, / Eternal Father." The child being called Mighty God and the Son being called Eternal Father are also a couplet. The mighty God is simply Jehovah God; the eternal Father is just another way of saying it. This means that the mighty God and the eternal Father form a pair poetically. This is to say that the eternal Father is the mighty God, just as the child is the Son and the Son is the child in the previous line.

As to His becoming a man, He is the child who was born of Mary in a manger. But as to His eternal divinity, He is the Son of God. This One who is the child and the Son is the mighty God and the eternal Father. Since Jesus is the child and the Son, He is the mighty God and the eternal Father. The infant Jesus who was born in a manger is the mighty God and the eternal Father. The child and the Son are one; the mighty God and the eternal Father are also one. Whether it be the child, the Son, the mighty God, or the eternal Father, they are all only one Person; they all refer to the all-inclusive Christ.

CHRIST COMING FROM THE POSITION OF THE CREATOR TO THE POSITION OF THE CREATURE

In 1934 Brother Nee held the third Overcomer Conference in Shanghai on Christ having the preeminence in all things. Both that dissenting one and I attended. I was the one who took notes of the message. Brother Nee asked me to organize my notes and publish them in the issue of *The Present Testimony* of March-April, 1934. There was even a note printed at the end of the message: "Spoken by Watchman Nee; recorded by Witness Lee." In this issue of *The Present Testimony* was an article entitled "God's Center or the Centrality and Universality of God." [Editor's note: This message has been included in *The Collected Works of Watchman Nee,* Set One, Volume 11, published by the Living Stream Ministry.] This message contains the following paragraph:

> The first thing in Christ's redemption is His incarnation. Christ was incarnated to be a man in order to come from the position of the Creator to the position of the creature. He had to take on a created body before He could die for man and for all things. There must first be Bethlehem before there can be Golgotha. There must first be the manger before there can be the cross. (*The Collected Works of Watchman Nee,* Set One, Volume 11, p. 740)

In this paragraph there is a line that says "to come from the position of the Creator to the position of the creature." This means that He is the Creator, but that in incarnation He as the Creator became a creature. Later, that dissenting brother translated these messages into English and translated this part as, "In becoming a man He steps down from the position of the Creator to the place of the created." In his translation, he completely changed the meaning of Brother Nee's words. What Brother Nee meant may be compared to a king who steps down from his royal position to a commoner's position; this means that the king becomes a commoner. However, the translator would not translate it this way. Rather, he changed it to say that the king steps down from his royal position to the place of the common people. This may be compared to the

Queen of England, who, when she goes to Hong Kong, goes to the place of the common people for a little visit. However, when the Lord Jesus became a man, He did not merely come to the place of the common people; rather, He came to the position of the common people to become a common person. The way that brother translated was not faithful to the original writing.

THE CHURCH BEING THE MYSTERY OF CHRIST

Now we come to the subject of this chapter: the mystery of Christ. The universe is a mystery, man is a mystery, and even more, God is a mystery. The Bible reveals these things very clearly, and there is no need for man to infer or grope. Then the Bible reveals another great mystery, which is the mystery of Christ. The mystery of Christ is the church. Colossians shows us that the mystery of God is Christ, while Ephesians shows us that the mystery of Christ is the church. These two books may be called sister books; one is on Christ and the other is on the church. All the "stories" of God are related to Christ, and all the "stories" of Christ are related to the church. The church came out of Christ; the church is also the expression of Christ. This is an exceedingly great mystery in the universe.

In the New Testament, we have the four Gospels which record the things of Christ's human life on the earth, showing us what kind of person Christ was. These four Gospels are biographies of Christ. After the four Gospels, the church began in the book of Acts. However, in the book of Acts we still cannot see the revelation and the story of the church. Only in the Epistles does Paul show us clearly how the church is the mystery of Christ and the story of Christ. This revelation was mainly written in the book of Ephesians.

From Ephesians 1 we can see that the church was chosen and predestinated by God before the foundation of the world. In time, because of man's fall, Christ came to redeem us who were chosen and predestinated by God. After Christ redeemed us, the Spirit came to seal us; that is, the Spirit seals us with God's life and nature and all that God is. The beginning of this sealing is our regeneration. When we believed in the Lord, the Spirit of God came to seal us. The first part of this sealing is regeneration. When the Spirit of God regenerated us, He sealed us with God's life so that we have God's life and nature within us. From that time the Spirit of God has been continuously sealing us within. This part of the sealing sanctifies us, makes us spiritual, and causes the elements of God to increase in us until we grow and mature in the divine life. This sealing of the Holy Spirit causes us to have an organic union with God. In this organic union, we enjoy God's rich life, which is Christ Himself, and we become the Body of Christ.

THE CHURCH BEING THE BODY OF CHRIST AS THE EXPRESSION OF CHRIST

This Christ was God who became flesh and who passed through death and resurrection. His resurrection was a work of God's power because it was God's power that raised Him from the dead and brought Him into ascension in the heavenlies, highly exalting Him to be far above all and giving Him to be Head over all things to the church.

This resurrection power of Christ not only enabled Him to ascend to heaven, to be far above all, and to become Head over all things; it also operates within us today. Because the Spirit of God operates in us, this power operates in us along with the Spirit of God. This power not only regenerates and sanctifies us but also transforms us, bringing us into an organic union with God. In this organic union we enjoy Christ's powerful life for us practically to become members of the Body of Christ. The aggregate of all the members of Christ is the Body of Christ, which is the church, the fullness of Christ, who fills all in all. This fullness is the expression of the Christ who fills all in all (Eph. 1:23).

The church is not an organization, nor is it merely an assembly formed by a group of the Lord's believers joining together. That may be a religious body but not the Body of Christ. The Body of Christ is an organism. As such, we have the life of God within us and the Spirit of God sealing us, step by step, with all that God is in Christ, that we may be sanctified and transformed and that we may experience the power that enabled Christ to rise from the dead, ascend to heaven, transcend all things, and be Head over all things. It is not in our natural life nor in our natural disposition nor in our own abilities and power and much less in our own merits, goodness, or good points that we become the Body of Christ. It is altogether through the sealing by the Spirit of God with God's life and nature that we are regenerated, sanctified, and transformed, thereby being fully united with Christ. Individually speaking, we have become the members of Christ; corporately speaking, we have become the Body of Christ. Therefore, the Body of Christ is not an organization but an organism.

All the stories of God are in Christ. God is in Christ, and Christ is the embodiment of God. After Christ's death and resurrection, all the stories of Christ are in the church. Today the church is the Body of Christ; Christ lives in this Body and is expressed through this Body. Hence, the church is a matter of Christ's life. The church has Christ as her life and everything. Just as God lived in Christ and was expressed through Christ, so Christ also lives in the church and is expressed through the church. The Head is Christ, and the Body is the church. The life of the Head is the life of the Body. All that the Head has is all that the Body has. In the Head there is God, and the Head is the expression of God; in the Body there is also God, and the Body is also the expression of God. All the stories of God are in Christ, and all the stories of Christ are in the church. In Christ we are not scattered; rather, we are one Body. There is nothing other than the Body that can express how intimate and inseparable our relationship is. This is an organic union.

THE CHURCH BEING THE NEW MAN

Ephesians 2:14-16 shows us that Christ's death on the cross abolished the barriers between the Jews and the Gentiles, breaking down the middle wall of partition between them, that in the salvation of the power of His life the two may become one Body, which is the one corporate new man, the church. In this new man, only Christ is all and in all (Col. 3:10-11).

Christ is also every part of this corporate new man (1 Cor. 12:12) and lives in every part (every member). He is the content and reality of this new man. This new man is the mystery and story of Christ, the all-inclusive One.

THE CHURCH ENJOYING THE RICHES OF CHRIST TO BECOME THE FULLNESS OF GOD

Ephesians 3 shows us that God wants to dispense the unsearchable riches of Christ into us to be our enjoyment day by day. Therefore, the apostle Paul prayed that God would grant us, according to the riches of His glory, to be strengthened with power through His Spirit into the inner man. Our inner man is our regenerated spirit, which has been mingled with the Holy Spirit into one spirit. God will strengthen us with power through His Spirit into our inner new man. This means that God wants us not to live by our outward, natural man nor by our soul—our mind, will, and emotion. God wants our whole being to enter into our regenerated spirit, into our spirit which has been mingled with the Holy Spirit as one, into our inner new man.

When we live in this way, Christ can then make His home in our hearts. When Christ thus makes His home in our hearts, His unsearchable riches become our enjoyment. Then we will be able to apprehend with all the saints how wide, long, high, and deep Christ is and how immeasurable He is. Therefore, at this stage, the riches of Christ are received and experienced by the church. Hence, all the stories of Christ are in the church, which enjoys all His riches. For this reason, the church becomes the mystery of Christ.

Verse 19 shows us that when we enjoy all the riches of Christ by being strengthened into our inner man and allowing Him to make His home in our hearts, the result is that we are filled with everything of God so that we become the fullness, the expression, of God.

The word *fullness* means to overflow and thereby become an expression. For example, when I pour milk into a cup, if I do not fill the cup, the milk will not be expressed. But if I continue to pour the milk until it fills the cup and even overflows the cup, this overflow will be the expression of the milk through the cup. Today, if the church has Christ without an overflow, the church cannot express Christ or God. We need to let the riches of Christ fill us completely even until they overflow. At this time, we will be not only the expression of Christ but also the expression of God. We will be not only the fullness of Christ but also the fullness of God.

THE CHURCH BEING MINGLED
WITH THE TRIUNE GOD TO BE ONE

In chapter four, Ephesians goes on to speak of the oneness of the Spirit. There it says that the Body is one and the Spirit is one, so the hope is also one. Now this Spirit is in the Body, and we are this Body. However, our bodies have not been transfigured yet. Therefore, we have a hope, which is that one day even our body of humiliation of the old creation will also be changed into a body of glory of the new creation. This means that at the Lord's coming, our body will be redeemed and transfigured into a glorious body. This is our hope. We have this hope of glory because of the Spirit, the Lord Himself, who is within us.

Ephesians 4 goes on to say that this one Body, which is made up of us, has only one Lord. We are joined to the Lord through faith and baptism. Through faith we receive the Lord into us, and through baptism we are immersed into Him. To believe is to enter into and have an organic union with the Lord. To be baptized is to end, to terminate, our all. Finally, this passage speaks of one God and Father of all, who is over all, through all, and in all.

All these matters show us that our being saved to become the church is altogether a matter of being completely mingled with the Triune God—the Spirit, the Lord, and the Father. For this reason, the church is the mystery of Christ, just as Christ is the mystery of God. Christ is one with God; also the church is one with Christ. The God in Christ has become the God in the church. The church is mingled as one with the Triune God.

THE CHURCH BEING THE BRIDE OF CHRIST

In chapter five, Ephesians goes on further to show us that

the church is not only the new man to fulfill God's will but also the bride, the counterpart, for Christ's satisfaction. To be sure, such a church will have been possessed by and saturated with the Triune God. At this stage, we enjoy the Triune God not only as grace and reality but also as love and light. We live in and enjoy God's love; we also live in and enjoy God's light. In this way all of our living and our walk become fully normal.

THE CHURCH BEING THE WARRIOR

In chapter six, the book of Ephesians shows us from another side that the church is also a warrior. As the mystery of Christ, the church is a warrior fighting for God's kingdom to destroy and trample on God's enemy, Satan. We become God's warriors not by ourselves but by being in Christ and by His power to take up the whole armor of God. Every part of the whole armor of God is Christ. We have the girdle of truth to gird our loins; this truth is Christ. We have the breastplate of righteousness to cover our conscience, and we also have the gospel of peace to shod our feet. This righteousness and this peace are also Christ. Then we have the shield of faith to protect our whole being. This faith is also Christ. Furthermore, we have the sword of the Spirit, which is the word of God, for us to attack the enemy. This word is also Christ. Christ is the whole armor of God for us to put on that we may be able to withstand the enemy, and having done all, to stand.

In conclusion, the book of Ephesians shows us that as the mystery of Christ, the church has Christ's life and nature and was raised up together and ascended together with Him. Furthermore, the church has the power of Christ operating within her, causing her to be far above all and become the Body of Christ, enjoying the unsearchable riches of Christ to become the fullness of Christ, the expression of Christ, which is also the fullness of God, the expression of God. This church is the new man to fulfill God's purpose, and she is also the bride to satisfy Christ's heart's desire. Furthermore, she is the spiritual warrior to withstand God's enemy and bring in God's kingdom. This is the mystery of Christ. The mystery of Christ is such a marvelous church.

CHAPTER FIVE

THE MYSTERY OF THE CHURCH

Scripture Reading: Eph. 1:23; 1 Tim. 3:15-16; Rev. 1:11, 20; 2:7; 19:7, 21:2, 9-10; 22:17

Prayer: O Lord, we prostrate ourselves to worship You. We worship You for Your grace and even more for Yourself. How glorious it is that You have come into us to be our life and everything. You are one with us, and we are one spirit with You. You have also made us Your glorious Body. Lord, we really worship You. This age is evil and is dark, yet You always shine upon us with Your light. You have separated us and placed us in this glorious position today to be Your golden lampstands shining forth in each locality. You have even made us Your dear bride to satisfy Your desire; we are flesh of Your flesh and bone of Your bones. We have become one Body with You in spirit. This Body is not only local but also universal. O Lord, we are full of praises within to You. We praise You that You are the Triune God and the Lord of all, the Lord of glory. Lord, may You fill us again with Yourself. May heaven and earth be joined, and may earth enter into heaven. We all shout with joy in You, "Jesus is Lord, Amen!"

THE MYSTERY OF THE CHURCH
BEING THE ULTIMATE MYSTERY IN THE UNIVERSE

In this chapter we want to see the last mystery, which is the mystery of the church. This mystery is in the universe and also in the Bible, especially the last book of the Bible— Revelation. This is the ultimate mystery.

Although this book has only five chapters, it encompasses the whole Bible. We are fellowshipping from Genesis 1 to Revelation 22: from God, heaven and earth, and man to Jesus

Christ, to the church—the golden lampstand, and finally to the holy city, New Jerusalem—the bride of the Lamb.

If we take a look at the Bible with a bird's-eye view, we will discover that the Bible opens by saying, "In the beginning God created the heavens and the earth" (Gen. 1:1). Genesis 1 begins by speaking of God, of heaven and earth, and then about the creation of man, particularly about the creation of a spirit in man. God stretched forth the heavens, laid the foundations of the earth, and formed the spirit of man within him (Zech. 12:1). The Chinese consider heaven, earth, and man as the three powers; the Bible also ranks man's spirit with heaven and earth. Hence, the Old Testament begins from God, passes through heaven and earth, and reaches man, even the spirit of man.

The New Testament, as a continuation of the Old Testament, begins with the four Gospels which are concerning the incarnated Jesus the Nazarene, whose human living on earth was a solid expression of God in Christ. After the four Gospels, there are the Acts and the Epistles concerning Christ being enlarged to become the church. Ephesians 1:22-23 tells us that Christ is the Head of the church, and the church is the Body of Christ, the expression of Christ's fullness. Then we come to Revelation, which opens by telling us that the seven golden lampstands are seven churches. This means that each local church equals one lampstand. Finally, at the end of Revelation, when the city of New Jerusalem appears, it is a huge golden lampstand, which is a great city on a great mountain. This great city is the beloved bride of Christ. How glorious! Revelation 21:2 says, "And I saw the holy city, New Jerusalem, coming down out of heaven from God, prepared as a bride adorned for her husband." When Christ returns, He will marry the church as His bride (Rev. 19:7). The New Jerusalem is the ultimate manifestation of this bride, the final fulfillment of that which is typified by Eve in Genesis 2.

The Bible covers six important items. The first item is God; the second item includes the heavens and the earth; the third item is man; the fourth item is Jesus Christ; the fifth item is the church, the golden lampstand; and the sixth item is the bride—the city, New Jerusalem. God, the Creator of the heavens and the earth, created man at the end of the process of His creation. However, what is important to God is neither the heavens nor the earth but man. Yet for man to exist, there surely is the need for the earth; moreover, for the earth to supply life, there surely is the need for the heavens. Hence, the heavens are for the earth, the earth is for man, and man is for God as His satisfaction.

The God who created all things came into the midst of men through His incarnation. This One who came was Jesus Christ. This Jesus Christ needed to be enlarged, and His enlargement is the church. The church shining brightly on the earth today is the golden lampstand. This golden lampstand has God as its substance, Christ as its form, and the Holy Spirit shining for its expression. In eternity, the ultimate manifestation of this church is the New Jerusalem, the beloved bride of Christ. Revelation 22:17 says, "And the Spirit and the bride say, Come!" The Spirit and the bride, having become one, speak together as one. God and man will become an eternal couple. Therefore, the New Jerusalem is the ultimate expression of God's entering into man. This is the story of the universe, the ultimate manifestation of the universe. God obtains an eternal and full expression in the man whom He created. This is the ultimate mystery in the universe—the mystery of the church.

THE CHURCH BEING CHRIST'S ORGANISM AND ENLARGEMENT

We have already seen that the church is the Body of Christ, the fullness of the One who fills all in all (Eph. 1:23). It is correct to say, according to the Greek word *ekklesia* for church, that the church is a group of people called out by the Lord to meet in the Lord's name, but this is too superficial and shallow. The church is not merely a called-out congregation. Such a congregation may be a human organization. However, the church is not a human organization but an organism with the life of Christ. For example, a table that is composed of a few pieces of wood is a lifeless thing, an organization. However, our human body, which is constituted with four limbs and many other parts, is an organism with life. It is something organic, something with life, and something living; it is not something formed by organization. So also is the church. The church is neither an organized group of people nor merely a kind of gathering. Rather, the church is Christ's organism, the Body with Christ as its life.

The Bible shows us that Christ with the church is one great person. Christ is the Head, and the church is the Body. From God's eternal view, in the universe there is only one great person—Christ with the church. In this universal great man, Christ is the Head and the church is the Body. Man's body is an organism, and only those parts that have an organic relationship with this body are the members of this body. We all know that to have a skin graft or an organ transplant in the human body, not only should the two lives be the same, but they should also be able to form an organic relationship with each other. This is even more true with the Body of Christ. Every part of the Body must have the life of Christ and an organic relationship with Christ. However, in today's so-called churches there are even false members. These false members do not belong to the Body of Christ. Today we are in the churches in the Lord's recovery, and we all have the life of Christ. However, if we do not live by Christ, we too will not have the reality of the church as the Body of Christ. This is because the church is altogether the organic Body of Christ.

Thank and praise the Lord that today our Lord Jesus is the life-giving Spirit! Once we believe in Him and receive Him as our Lord, He enters into us as the Spirit to be our life and life supply. When we live according to and by this Spirit day by day, we are the genuine and living members of the Body of Christ. We all are living members, and the Spirit within us echoes from one to another and flows from one to another; moreover, there are no distinctions and no differences among us. This is the church, which is the Body of Christ, as mentioned in Ephesians 1:23.

Ephesians 1:23 also says that the church is the fullness of the One who fills all in all. The One who fills all in all is our Lord Jesus Christ. The church is His overflow and enlargement. When the Lord Jesus was on earth, if He was in

Bethlehem, He could not be in Nazareth; if He was in Nazareth, He could not be in Samaria; and if He was in Samaria, He could not be in Jerusalem. Today, however, He has been enlarged into the church, so He is everywhere on the whole earth. This is the enlargement and the overflow of Christ.

THE CHURCH BEING THE HOUSE OF GOD
APPEARING IN LOCALITIES

First Timothy 3:15-16 says, "The house of God, which is the church of the living God, the pillar and base of the truth. And confessedly, great is the mystery of godliness: He who was manifested in the flesh." The church is the house of God, the manifestation of God in the flesh. The church is also the firm pillar and base to support the truth. The church has the pure and high truths, and it is the place where God speaks. God is speaking in the church today, so it is only in the church that people can receive the pure and unadulterated truths.

Revelation 1:11 tells us that John was in spirit and heard a loud voice saying, "What you see write in a scroll and send it to the seven churches: to Ephesus and to Smyrna and to Pergamos and to Thyatira and to Sardis and to Philadelphia and to Laodicea." According to what is mentioned here, the written scroll being sent to the seven churches equals its being sent to the seven cities. This shows clearly that the practice of the church life in the early days was the practice of having one church for one city, one city with only one church. The manifestation of the church should be in localities, and it should be one city with one church.

The church is the house of God, the Body of Christ, and the fullness of the One who fills all in all. However, the church is expressed locally, one church for one city. There should never be more than one church in any one city. If there are two or more churches in a city, that is division. Yet, today there are many so-called churches in one city; this is division.

THE CHURCH BEING THE GOLDEN LAMPSTAND

Revelation 1:12 says, "And when I turned,...I saw seven golden lampstands." Then verse 20 says, "The mystery of...the seven golden lampstands...the seven churches." This clearly tells us that a local church is a golden lampstand. Some say that a lampstand is for shining and that in this dark age today, the church shines as a golden lampstand. Although it is right to say this, the golden lampstand is not so simple. We need to read the Bible and find the entire history of the golden lampstand so that we may understand its significance.

We know that the revelation in the Bible develops progressively. The seeds of the divine revelation are sown mostly in the first few books of the Bible, and then they are gradually developed in the succeeding books until Revelation, where the harvest is reaped. The revelation concerning the golden lampstand is no exception. The seed of the revelation concerning the golden lampstand is sown in Exodus 25. Then in 1 Kings 7 it sprouts; in Zechariah 4 it is developed; and finally in Revelation it is harvested.

The Golden Lampstand Being the Solid Expression of the Triune God

Exodus 25 mentions that the golden lampstand is beaten out of one piece of pure gold. It has a shaft with six branches going out from its sides, three branches on the right side and three branches on the left side. On the branches there are three layers—the cups, the calyxes, and the blossoming buds; in addition, there are the lamps. This picture first shows us that the substance of the golden lampstand is pure gold; second, that the one piece of gold is beaten into a golden lampstand with a form; and third, that the golden lampstand has seven lamps. The meaning is this: First, according to biblical typology, gold signifies the nature of God. God's nature is unique, divine, pure, unalterable, and lasting. Therefore, the emphasis here is that the pure gold as the substance of the lampstand signifies the Father as the nature of the golden lampstand. Second, the form of the lampstand signifies Christ. The incarnated Christ is God's form, God's solid expression: "For in Him dwells all the fullness of the Godhead bodily" (Col. 2:9). Christ is the impress of God's substance (Heb. 1:3) and the image of the invisible God (Col. 1:15). Christ is also the only begotten Son in the bosom of the

Father who declared God (John 1:18). John 14 even tells us that when we see the Son, we also see the Father because the Son is the solid expression of the Father. Hence, the lampstand here signifies the Son who declared the Father. Third, the golden lampstand has seven lamps. Concerning this, we cannot find the answer in Exodus. We need to look at Zechariah and Revelation together to understand the significance of the seven lamps.

Zechariah 4 says that there are two olive trees beside the golden lampstand. The prophet Zechariah asked, "What are these, sir?" (v. 4). The angel answered, "Not by might nor by power, but by My Spirit, says Jehovah of hosts" (v. 6). Here, therefore, the revelation of the Spirit is implied. Exodus only mentions the golden lampstand which signifies Christ; it does not mention the olive oil which typifies the Spirit. It is not until Zechariah 4 that there is a further revelation—a revelation concerning the Spirit. Furthermore, it shows us that the seven lamps are the seven eyes of Jehovah. Revelation 4:5 tells us that the seven lamps before the throne are the seven Spirits of God, and Revelation 5:6 tells us that the seven eyes of the Lamb are the seven Spirits of God. By putting together these passages, we can see that the seven lamps of the golden lampstand in the book of Zechariah are the seven Spirits of God in Revelation. Hence, the seven lamps signify the expression and shining of the Spirit. Thus, this golden lampstand not only has the substance of the Father, the form of the Son, but even more the expression of the Spirit. In other words, the testimony of the church is the solid expression of the Triune God.

According to the record in Revelation 1, we see that where the church is, there is the golden lampstand. Where the church is, there are the substance of God and the riches of Christ, and there are also God's dispensing, transmission, supply, and even judgment. Every local church is an embodiment of the Triune God—the Father, the Son, and the Spirit. When people come to the church, they can sense that God is here, Christ is here, and the Spirit is here. This is the Father, the Son, and the Spirit operating, shining, and being manifested and expressed here. Such a church is the golden lampstand.

THE CHURCH BEING THE BRIDE OF CHRIST

Revelation 19:7 says, "Let us rejoice and exult, and let us give the glory to Him, for the marriage of the Lamb has come, and His wife has made herself ready." The bride refers to the saints throughout the ages who are the overcomers reigning with Christ in the millennial kingdom. The readiness of the bride indicates growth and maturity in life. When we are saturated by the Triune God so that He flows out of us, we are completely built and fitted together to become the glorious church, the beloved bride of the Lord Jesus.

"The marriage of the Lamb has come." Who will the Lamb marry? The Catholic Church? No! Only the golden lampstand can be the bride of Christ. We need to live out the life of Christ. We do not care for even any goodness that comes out of ourselves, not to mention any wickedness that comes out of ourselves. We care for the tree of life; we care for the Triune God; and we care for Jesus Christ as the all-inclusive Spirit. Whether we are at home with our spouses and children or in the church meetings with the brothers and sisters, we all need to live out Christ. If we live by Christ, then what we live out is the pure gold that shines forth the light; then we can become the bride of Christ to satisfy His desire.

THE CONSUMMATE MANIFESTATION OF THE CHURCH BEING THE NEW JERUSALEM

Revelation 21:2 says, "And I saw the holy city, New Jerusalem, coming down out of heaven from God, prepared as a bride adorned for her husband." The bride here refers to all the saints, both in the Old Testament and in the New Testament, as the counterpart of Christ in eternity.

Revelation 21:9-10 also tells us that the angel said to John, "Come here; I will show you the bride, the wife of the Lamb." John was carried away in spirit onto a great and high mountain where he saw the holy city, New Jerusalem, coming down out of heaven. This tells us that the bride of Christ is a city—the New Jerusalem. Verses 12 to 20 go on to tell us the dimensions of the holy city itself and of its wall. The New Jerusalem is a cube; its length, its breadth, and its height are equal, each side being twelve thousand stadia, which equals about twenty-three hundred kilometers; it looks like a great and high mountain. This city is built upon twelve foundations, and on them are the names of the twelve apostles of the Lamb, representing all the New Testament saints. This city also has twelve gates, on which are written the names of the twelve tribes of Israel, representing all the Old Testament saints. Hence, the New Jerusalem is the aggregate of all the saints in both the Old Testament and the New Testament. This is the ultimate manifestation of the church. What a mystery!

The New Jerusalem is built with three kinds of material. The city proper with its street is of pure gold, the twelve gates are pearls, and the wall and foundations are various kinds of precious stones. We have already said that gold signifies the Father's nature, indicating that the Father is the substance of this city. Pearls signify the death and resurrection of the Son, indicating that His overcoming death which terminates everything of the old creation and His glorious resurrection which imparts new life become the gates of the New Jerusalem for us to enter in. Precious stones signify the transforming and sanctifying work of the Holy Spirit, indicating that under the transforming work of the Holy Spirit, we, the saved and regenerated ones, become precious stones as the materials for God's building. Hence, the city, the New Jerusalem, is the enlarged embodiment of the Triune God. The church today is the golden lampstand which expresses the Triune God in each locality in this age. The ultimate consummation of the church is the New Jerusalem, which will express the Triune God in the whole universe in eternity.

Revelation 22:17 says, "And the Spirit and the bride say, Come!" In Revelation 2 and 3, it is the Spirit speaking to the churches (2:7, 11, 17, 29; 3:6, 13, 22), but at the end of the whole Bible it is the Spirit and the bride speaking together. The Spirit is the ultimate consummation of the Triune God as the Bridegroom; the bride is the ultimate consummation of the redeemed man. After this universal marriage, the Triune

God and redeemed man are not separate. They do not speak separately, but the two have become one couple, so there is the speaking of the Spirit and the bride together. Hallelujah, God and man are mingled and united to become the universal and eternal couple, moving together and speaking together! This is the accomplishment of God's ultimate goal.

The five great mysteries in the Bible are first, the mystery of the universe, which is God; second, the mystery of man, which is also God; third, the mystery of God, which is Christ; fourth, the mystery of Christ, which is the church; and fifth, the mystery of the church, which is the organism of Christ as the overflow and enlargement of Christ, the house of God, the golden lampstand, the bride, and the New Jerusalem. This is the ultimate mystery in the universe. Today, God is moving on in every place throughout the whole earth. Every local church is a mystery as the organism of Christ, the enlargement and overflow of Christ, the house of God, the golden lampstand, and the bride. Finally, in eternity we will all become the ultimate expression of God—the New Jerusalem. Then God will achieve His ultimate goal in the universe.

ABOUT THE AUTHOR

Witness Lee was born in 1905 in northern China and raised in a Christian family. At age 19 he was fully captured for Christ and immediately consecrated himself to preach the gospel for the rest of his life. Early in his service, he met Watchman Nee, a renowned preacher, teacher, and writer. Witness Lee labored together with Watchman Nee under his direction. In 1934 Watchman Nee entrusted Witness Lee with the responsibility for his publication operation, called the Shanghai Gospel Bookroom.

Prior to the Communist takeover in 1949, Witness Lee was sent by Watchman Nee and his other co-workers to Taiwan to ensure that the things delivered to them by the Lord would not be lost. Watchman Nee instructed Witness Lee to continue the former's publishing operation abroad as the Taiwan Gospel Bookroom, which has been publicly recognized as the publisher of Watchman Nee's works outside China. Witness Lee's work in Taiwan manifested the Lord's abundant blessing. From a mere 350 believers, newly fled from the mainland, the churches in Taiwan grew to 20,000 in five years.

In 1962 Witness Lee felt led of the Lord to come to the United States, settling in California. During his 35 years of service in the U.S., he ministered in weekly meetings and weekend conferences, delivering several thousand spoken messages. Much of his speaking has since been published as over 400 titles. Many of these have been translated into over fourteen languages. He gave his last public conference in February 1997 at the age of 91.

He leaves behind a prolific presentation of the truth in the Bible. His major work, *Life-study of the Bible,* comprises over 25,000 pages of commentary on every book of the Bible from the perspective of the believers' enjoyment and experience of God's divine life in Christ through the Holy Spirit. Witness Lee was the chief editor of a new translation of the New Testament into Chinese called the Recovery Version and directed the translation of the same into English. The Recovery Version also appears in a number of other languages. He provided an extensive body of footnotes, outlines, and spiritual cross references. A radio broadcast of his messages can be heard on Christian radio stations in the United States. In 1965 Witness Lee founded Living Stream Ministry, a non-profit corporation, located in Anaheim, California, which officially presents his and Watchman Nee's ministry.

Witness Lee's ministry emphasizes the experience of Christ as life and the practical oneness of the believers as the Body of Christ. Stressing the importance of attending to both these matters, he led the churches under his care to grow in Christian life and function. He was unbending in his conviction that God's goal is not narrow sectarianism but the Body of Christ. In time, believers began to meet simply as the church in their localities in response to this conviction. In recent years a number of new churches have been raised up in Russia and in many eastern European countries.

OTHER BOOKS PUBLISHED BY
Living Stream Ministry

Titles by Witness Lee:

Abraham—Called by God	0-7363-0359-6
The Experience of Life	0-87083-417-7
The Knowledge of Life	0-87083-419-3
The Tree of Life	0-87083-300-6
The Economy of God	0-87083-415-0
The Divine Economy	0-87083-268-9
God's New Testament Economy	0-87083-199-2
The World Situation and God's Move	0-87083-092-9
Christ vs. Religion	0-87083-010-4
The All-inclusive Christ	0-87083-020-1
Gospel Outlines	0-87083-039-2
Character	0-87083-322-7
The Secret of Experiencing Christ	0-87083-227-1
The Life and Way for the Practice of the Church Life	0-87083-785-0
The Basic Revelation in the Holy Scriptures	0-87083-105-4
The Crucial Revelation of Life in the Scriptures	0-87083-372-3
The Spirit with Our Spirit	0-87083-798-2
Christ as the Reality	0-87083-047-3
The Central Line of the Divine Revelation	0-87083-960-8
The Full Knowledge of the Word of God	0-87083-289-1
Watchman Nee—A Seer of the Divine Revelation ...	0-87083-625-0

Titles by Watchman Nee:

How to Study the Bible	0-7363-0407-X
God's Overcomers	0-7363-0433-9
The New Covenant	0-7363-0088-0
The Spiritual Man 3 volumes	0-7363-0269-7
Authority and Submission	0-7363-0185-2
The Overcoming Life	1-57593-817-0
The Glorious Church	0-87083-745-1
The Prayer Ministry of the Church	0-87083-860-1
The Breaking of the Outer Man and the Release ...	1-57593-955-X
The Mystery of Christ	1-57593-954-1
The God of Abraham, Isaac, and Jacob	0-87083-932-2
The Song of Songs	0-87083-872-5
The Gospel of God 2 volumes	1-57593-953-3
The Normal Christian Church Life	0-87083-027-9
The Character of the Lord's Worker	1-57593-322-5
The Normal Christian Faith	0-87083-748-6
Watchman Nee's Testimony	0-87083-051-1

Available at
Christian bookstores, or contact Living Stream Ministry
2431 W. La Palma Ave. • Anaheim, CA 92801
1-800-549-5164 • www.livingstream.com